AF584446

WOMEN
IN
GREAT
AUSSIE
SPORTS
WOMEN'S
RUGBY
TONY LA TORRACA
REDBACK
publishing

First Published 2026 by
Redback Publishing
Suite 6, 13a Narabang Way,
Belrose NSW 2085
Australia

www.redbackpublishing.com
orders@redbackpublishing.com

ISBN 978-1-761401-90-9

Author: Tony La Torraca
Editor: Emma Elias
Designer: Redback Publishing

Original illustrations © Redback Publishing 2026
Originated by Redback Publishing

Acknowledgements
Abbreviations: l—left, r—right, b—bottom, t—top, c—centre, m—middle
We would like to thank the following for permission to reproduce photographs: (Images © shutterstock, Alamy)
Cover - Volodymyr Melnyk / Alamy, p2-3 - Cam Laird / Shutterstock.com, p4tr - By Sam Hood - State Library of New South Wales, Australia, Public Domain, https://commons.wikimedia.org/w/index.php?curid=6822647, p4b - IOIO Images / Shutterstock.com, p5tr - Elsie Kibue / Alamy, p5bc - Richard Milnes via Alamy, p6tl - Hyserb / Shutterstock.com, p6br - IOIO Images / Shutterstock.com, p7tl - Hyserb / Shutterstock.com, p7br - Action Plus Sports Images / Alamy, p8tl - atsportphoto / Shutterstock.com, p8br - Hyserb / Shutterstock.com, p9tr - IOIO Images / Alamy, p9br - alberto gardin / Shutterstock.com, p10br - Hyserb / Shutterstock.com, p12tl - Action Plus Sports Images / Alamy, p13br - PA Images / Alamy, p14tl - IOIO Images / Shutterstock.com, p14br - Hyserb / Shutterstock.com, p15tr - IOIO Images / Shutterstock.com, p16br - UK Sports Pics Ltd / Alamy, p17br - UK Sports Pics Ltd / Alamy, p18tl - Joe Ng / Alamy, p18m - IOIO Images / Shutterstock.com, p19tr - IOIO Images / Shutterstock.com, p20tr - Grindstone Media Group / Shutterstock.com, p20b - Feroz Khan / Alamy, p21tr - Hyserb / Shutterstock.com, p21bl - IOIO Images / Shutterstock.com, p22tr - IOIO Images / Shutterstock.com, p23tr - Hyserb / Shutterstock.com, p23bl - PA Images / Alamy, p24tr - Oleksandr Osipov / Shutterstock.com, p24bl - Suhaimi Sulaiman / Shutterstock.com, p25bl - IOIO Images / Shutterstock.com, p25br - Henry Saint John / Shutterstock.com, p25mr - IOIO Images / Shutterstock.com, p25tr - IOIO Images / Shutterstock.com, p26ml - IOIO Images / Shutterstock.com, p26br - Victor Velter / Shutterstock.com, p30tr - IOIO Images / Shutterstock.com, p31tr - IOIO Images / Shutterstock.com, p32 - IOIO Images / Shutterstock.com

A catalogue record for this book is available from the National Library of Australia

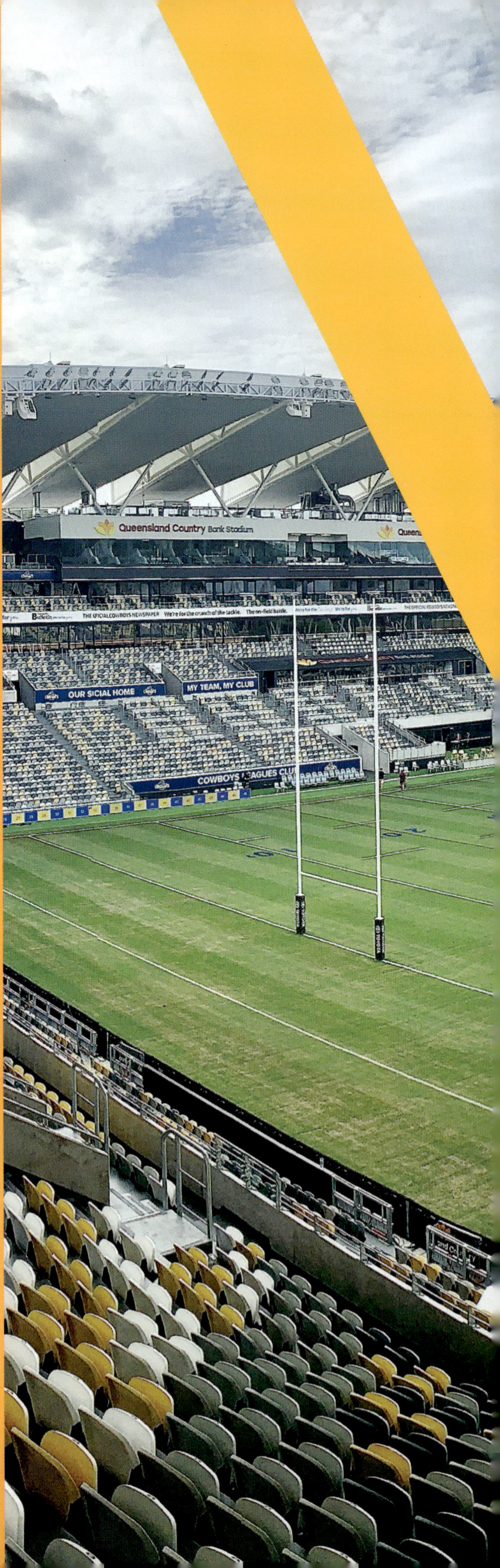

CONTENTS

PLAYER PROFILES

HISTORICAL BACKGROUND

Women's rugby union team in New South Wales, 1930s

While rugby union was introduced to Australia in the late 19th century, it took several decades before women began to carve their own space within the sport.

The first recorded women's rugby matches in Australia took place in 1930 but did not gain much momentum. It was during this decade that women began to organise informal games, primarily in New South Wales and Queensland, where rugby union had already cemented its popularity amongst men.

As the 1990s approached, women's rugby in Australia began to gain more structure. The establishment of formal competitions and the formation of women's rugby clubs provided a platform for the sport to flourish. In 1991, the Australian Women's Rugby Union (AWRU) was formed, marking a significant milestone in the sport's development.

The international scene also beckoned, with the inaugural Women's Rugby World Cup held in 1991 in Wales. Although Australia did not participate in the first tournament, the event sparked a growing interest in the international women's rugby circuit. By 1994, Australia fielded its first national women's team, the Wallaroos, who competed in the second Women's Rugby World Cup in Scotland.

Rugby 7s, with its fast-paced and dynamic style, provided an additional avenue for women to showcase their talents. The inclusion of women's rugby 7s in the 2016 Rio Olympics further propelled the sport into the limelight.

Women's rugby in Australia continues to thrive, with the Wallaroos and the national 7s team achieving remarkable success on the international stage.

The Australian Wallaroos

PIONEERS

Nicole Beck became a household name in the rugby community. Her ability to read the game and execute plays with precision made her a formidable opponent and an inspiring role model for aspiring players.

Another pioneer in the sport is Sharni Williams who first played 15s for Australia prior to joining the international 7s circuit. Williams' influence extends beyond her athletic achievements; she has been a vocal advocate for women's sports. Her efforts have not only elevated the status of women playing 7s in Australia but have also inspired countless young women to pursue their dreams in sports.

Chloe Dalton is another key figure whose impact on the sport has been profound. Dalton's versatility on the field, combined with her strategic thinking, has been a significant asset to the Australian team.

Bronnie Mackintosh was instrumental in establishing the Hong Kong, Darwin, and Sevens by the Sea tournaments. Bronnie, who plays both league and union internationally, continued to play 15s rugby into her fifties. She is the current CEO and founder of Girls on Fire.

Nicole Beck

Sharni Williams

Charlotte Caslick was born in Brisbane, and is the country's longest-serving women's rugby 7s player, with a decade-long career spanning over 300 games.

Australia's all-time leading try-scorer, Caslick made history in 2016 as a part of the gold medal winning team that defeated New Zealand in the final in Rio.

She has been influential in leading the charge to overall series titles in 2015-16, 2018, 2022 and more recently in the 2023-2024 season, winning the Madrid Sevens Grand Final. Widely regarded as the world's best rugby 7s player, Caslick is signed with Rugby Australia until at least the end of 2026.

Her journey from local club matches to the global stage is a testament to her unwavering dedication and exceptional talent.

Caslick's playing style is a mesmerising blend of speed and strategy, a dynamic force that often leaves both opponents and spectators in awe. Her ability to read the game with an almost intuitive understanding sets her apart as a playmaker of remarkable skill. Whether darting through defensive lines with her electrifying pace or orchestrating plays with her keen eye for opportunity, Caslick's influence on the game is undeniable.

RUGBY FOR EVERYONE

Since 2019, there have been huge improvements and changes to the accessibility of rugby programs in communities and cultures that weren't traditionally involved in the sport. With new approaches to the way clubs operate, and more inclusive methods of teaching the game, a much wider age of girls can now play rugby. There are more opportunities and game options, including touch rugby, 7-a-side and 15s, and there has been a huge growth of girls and women playing rugby.

FIRST COMPETITIONS

In 1994, the Wallaroos achieved a significant breakthrough by hosting their first international test match against New Zealand.

The establishment of the Australian Women's Sevens team in 2008 marked a significant expansion of the women's rugby program. This new format, characterised by its fast pace and dynamic gameplay, quickly captured the imagination of fans and players alike. The team's dedication and hard work paid off when they qualified for the 2016 Rio Olympics, marking an historic moment for women's rugby in Australia. They achieved a monumental victory by securing the gold medal. In addition to their Olympic success, the Australian Women's Sevens team has consistently performed well in the World Rugby Women's Sevens Series. Their victories in multiple series titles have solidified their reputation as a formidable force in international women's rugby.

The Wallaroos have also continued to make strides in the 15s format, with notable performances in subsequent World Cups.

Michaela Lea Leonard plays at lock position for the Wallaroos and competed at the recent Rugby World Cup in New Zealand. She previously played for the Brumbies before joining the Western Force in the Super W competition.

Leonard made her debut for Australia against Japan in 2019. In 2021, she was named as captain of the Brumbies for the 2021 Super W season.

She was named in Australia's squad for the 2022 Pacific Four Series in New Zealand and was selected in the Wallaroos squad for a two-test series against the Black Ferns at the Laurie O'Reilly Cup. She was selected in the team again for the delayed 2022 Rugby World Cup in New Zealand. In 2023, she signed with the Western Force Super W season.

PLAYER PROFILE

MICHAELA LEA LEONARD

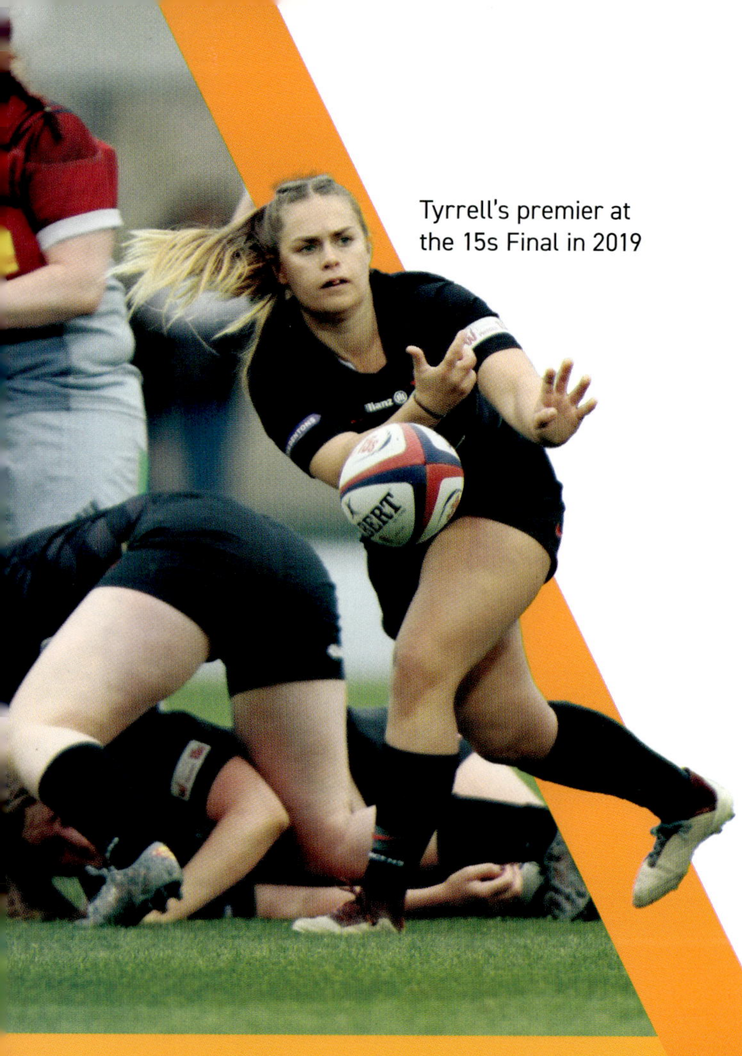

Tyrrell's premier at the 15s Final in 2019

THE 15s AND 7s FORMATS

The 15s and 7s formats are characterised by a blend of seasoned players and emerging stars. The 15s game, known for its strategic depth and physicality, has seen significant growth in recent years. This expansion is fuelled by increased participation at the grassroots (foundational) level, as well as enhanced support from national and regional rugby bodies. The commitment to developing female rugby talent is evident in the establishment of more structured pathways, allowing young players to transition smoothly from junior leagues to professional levels.

In the 7s format, agility, speed and tactical prowess take centre stage. Australia's Women's Rugby Sevens team has carved out a formidable reputation on the international stage. Their achievements have not only brought prestige but have also inspired a new generation of athletes, eager to don the green and gold jersey.

INTRODUCTION TO RUGBY 7s

Known for its fast-paced action, 7s is played with seven players per team, as opposed to the traditional fifteen, on the same size pitch. This format results in a game that is not only quicker but also demands exceptional athleticism, agility and strategic acumen from its players. Originating in Melrose, Scotland, in the late 19th century, rugby 7s has evolved into a globally recognised sport, culminating in its inclusion in the Olympic Games.

Matches are typically played over two halves of seven minutes each, with a brief halftime break, making the entire contest a brisk and intense affair. Due to fewer players being on the field, there is more open space, which creates opportunities for spectacular runs, evasive manoeuvres and tactical plays. These all contribute to the sport's thrilling unpredictability.

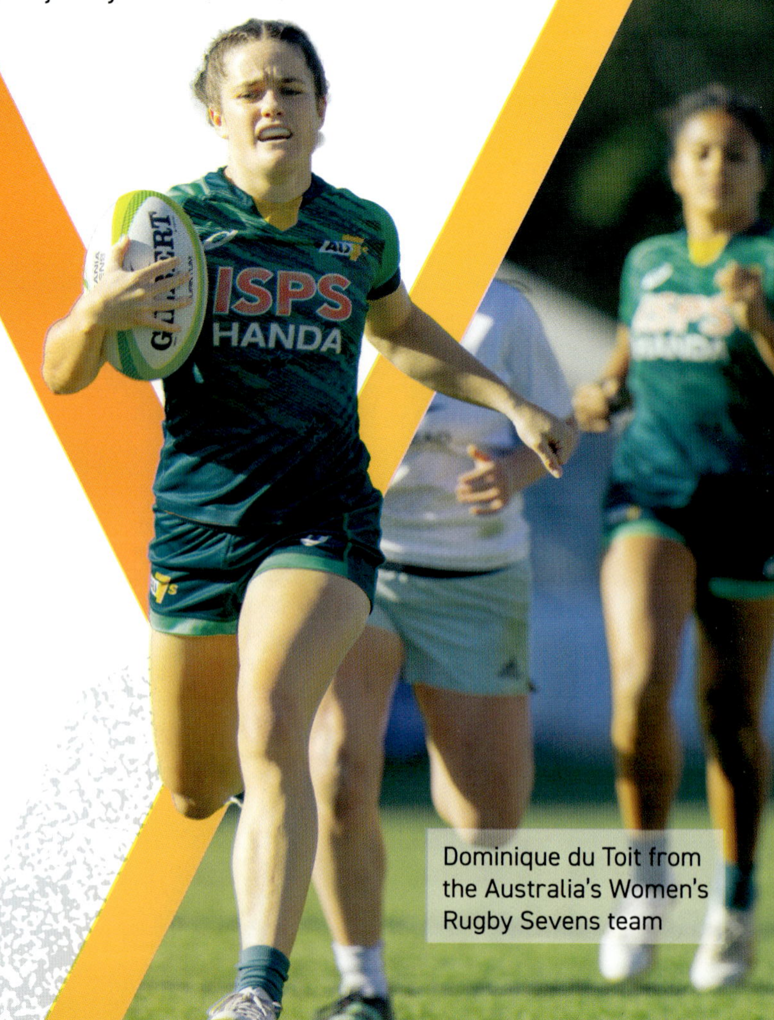

Dominique du Toit from the Australia's Women's Rugby Sevens team

Alysia Lefau-Fakaosilea is a promising New Zealand-born 7s young gun who moved to Queensland with her family during Australia's gold medal win in Rio, 2016.

Lefau-Fakaosilea went on to play for the Wallaroos in 2019, before moving into the Aussie 7s squad.

The ferocious speedster made her 7s debut against the Black Ferns in 2021 and was later called into the Tokyo Olympics squad. A shoulder injury hindered Lefau-Fakaosilea for most of the 2023-2024 season of the SVNS world series before she unfortunately ruptured her ACL at training on the eve of the Paris Olympics.

PLAYER PROFILE

ALYSIA LEFAU-FAKAOSILEA

Australia's women's rugby teams, both in the 15s and 7s formats, have etched their names onto the world stage through their participation in major competitions. These tournaments serve as not only a platform for showcasing their talent, but also as a crucible for honing their skills against the best in the world. The World Rugby Women's Sevens Series and the Rugby World Cup are two of the most significant events that have shaped the trajectory of women's rugby in Australia.

The World Rugby Women's Sevens Series stands as a premier international circuit where the Australian team has consistently excelled. It is a global tour that brings together the top teams from around the world to compete in a series of tournaments held in various countries. The Australian Women's Sevens team has consistently been a formidable force in this series.

On the other hand, the Rugby World Cup, held every four years, is the pinnacle of rugby union competition. For the Wallaroos, this tournament represents the ultimate test of endurance, skill and strategy.

RUGBY 7s IN THE OLYMPICS

The Australian Women's Rugby Sevens team's debut at the Rio Olympics in 2016 was nothing short of spectacular. Their performance was a masterclass in rugby 7s, characterised by swift movement, strategic positioning, and a relentless drive to dominate their opponents. The culmination of their efforts won them a well-deserved gold medal. As the Olympic flame continues to burn bright, the Australian Women's Rugby Sevens team remains committed to their mission of excellence.

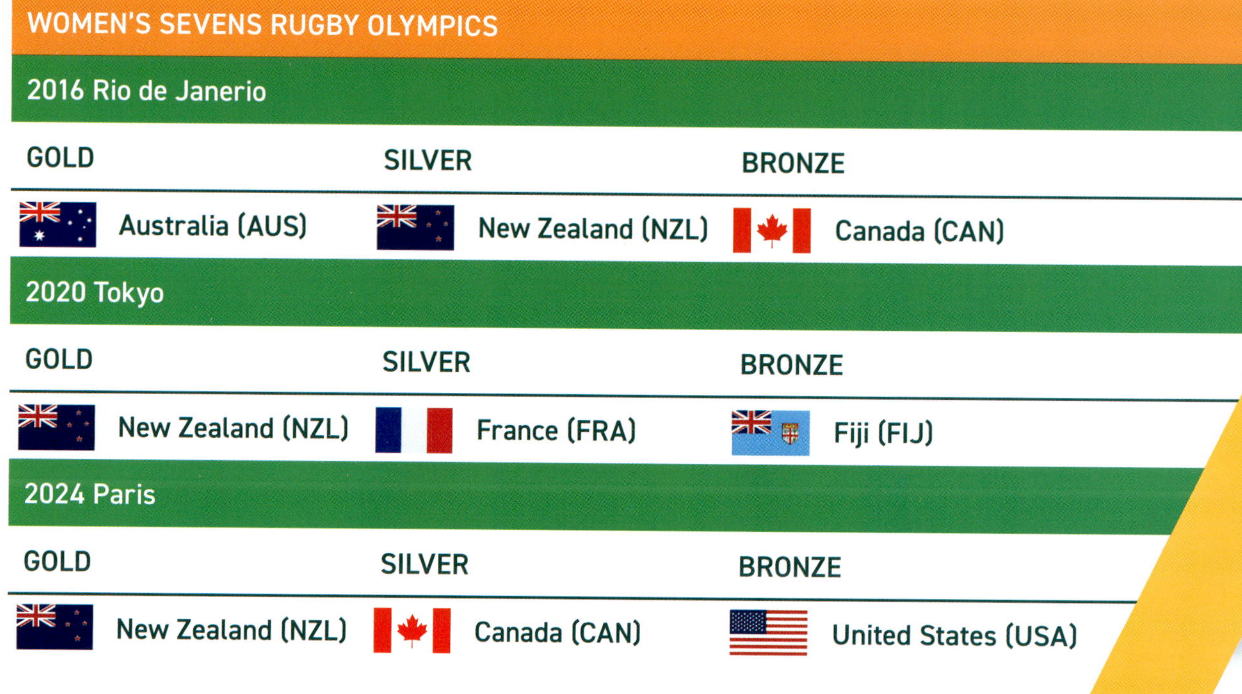

WOMEN'S SEVENS RUGBY OLYMPICS		
2016 Rio de Janerio		
GOLD	SILVER	BRONZE
Australia (AUS)	New Zealand (NZL)	Canada (CAN)
2020 Tokyo		
GOLD	SILVER	BRONZE
New Zealand (NZL)	France (FRA)	Fiji (FIJ)
2024 Paris		
GOLD	SILVER	BRONZE
New Zealand (NZL)	Canada (CAN)	United States (USA)

MODERN ICONS

Modern Icons and world rugby players of the year have been Debby Hodgkinson, Emilee Cherry, Charlotte Caslick and Maddison Levi.

Among these icons is also Sharni Williams, whose presence on the field is nothing short of electrifying. Williams has played a pivotal role in shaping the success of the Australian Women's Rugby Sevens team. As a captain, her leadership transcends the game, inspiring teammates and fans alike with her unwavering commitment to excellence.

In the 15s format, a notable player is Cheryl McAfee (née Soon) who captained both 7s and 15s in two World Cups. She led Australia's women to a piece of history as the first Rugby World Cup Sevens champions after they dramatically beat New Zealand 15-10 in sudden-death extra-time in Dubai.

Charlotte Caslick

COACHES

The impact of coaches is key to the success stories of many players who have risen to prominence on the international stage. They attribute their achievements to the guidance and support received from these influential figures. The relationship between players and their coaches and mentors is built on trust and mutual respect, forming a strong foundation that propels the entire team towards excellence.

In essence, the coaches and mentors of Australia's Women's Rugby 15s and 7s are more than just trainers or advisors; they are the guiding forces that shape the future of the sport. Their dedication and passion inspire not only the players but the entire rugby community, ensuring that the legacy of Australian Women's Rugby continues to thrive and evolve.

For the 15s, successful coaches include John Manenti, Ian Walsh and Scott Bowen. Champion coaches for the 7s are Bronnie Mackintosh, Selena Tranter and Tui Ormsby.

MEDIA AND PUBLICITY

Television broadcasts serve as a primary vehicle for showcasing the thrilling matches of Australian Women's Rugby. Major networks have recognised the appeal of the sport, providing extensive coverage that highlights not only the games but also the personal stories of the athletes. Slow-motion replays, expert commentary, and behind-the-scenes glimpses enrich the viewing experience, making it accessible and engaging for a diverse audience.

Social media platforms have emerged as powerful tools in the arsenal of media publicity for Australian Women's Rugby. Through platforms like Instagram, X and Facebook, athletes can share their journeys, training regimens and personal insights directly with their followers.

Print media, though often overshadowed by digital platforms, remains a vital component in the publicity landscape.

Maddison Levi is a current player for the Australian Women's Sevens team. Levi is an explosive try-scorer from the Gold Coast who made her 7s debut at the Tokyo Olympic Games in 2021. Levi grew up a talented dancer before starting a junior career in rugby. She played AFLW for the Gold Coast Suns briefly until moving back to 7s during her schooling at Miami State High School.

After scoring 14 tries in Paris, it is no wonder that Australia's Maddison Levi is the 2024 Sevens Player of the Year.

Levi's journey into the world of rugby 7s is a tale of raw talent refined through relentless dedication. From a young age, her athletic prowess was evident. Her early years were marked by a passion for competition, a drive that saw her excel in various athletic disciplines before committing to the fast-paced, high-stakes world of rugby 7s.

On the field, Levi's performance is characterised by her exceptional speed and agility. Her ability to read the game, anticipate plays, and position herself strategically has made her an invaluable asset to the team.

NEXT GEN 7s

The Next Gen 7s Series will be integrated into the wider community of women and girls' 7s events.

Rugby Australia Director of High-Performance, Peter Horne said, "Performance Pathways are critical in ensuring High Performance programs are successful at the highest levels of the game. The Next Gen 7s competition provides the platform and opportunity for our future talented players to be exposed to high level competition."

Fresh off breaking the record for most tries scored at an Olympic Games, two-time Olympian Maddison Levi said she was eager to support all teams after playing previously in similar tournaments.

Playing in tournaments like the Next Gen 7s allows young players to compete against other talent coming through the Australian 7s system.

ROLE OF SCHOOLS AND UNIVERSITIES

Schools and universities play a pivotal role in nurturing and developing talent for both the 15s and 7s formats. This inclusion not only promotes physical activity but also instils core values such as teamwork, discipline and resilience in young players. Teachers and coaches play a vital role, often going beyond the confines of their duties to inspire and mentor students. Their dedication is evident in the increasing number of school teams participating in inter-school competitions, which serve as a breeding ground for talent discovery and development.

The youth programs are meticulously designed to cater to various age groups, ensuring that the sport is not only about competition but also enjoyment and personal growth. These programs emphasise skill development, with a keen focus on fundamental techniques such as passing, tackling and strategic play.

Universities further extend the pathway for women in rugby by offering advanced training facilities and competitive environments. These institutions often host inter-university tournaments, which are crucial for identifying and developing young talent.

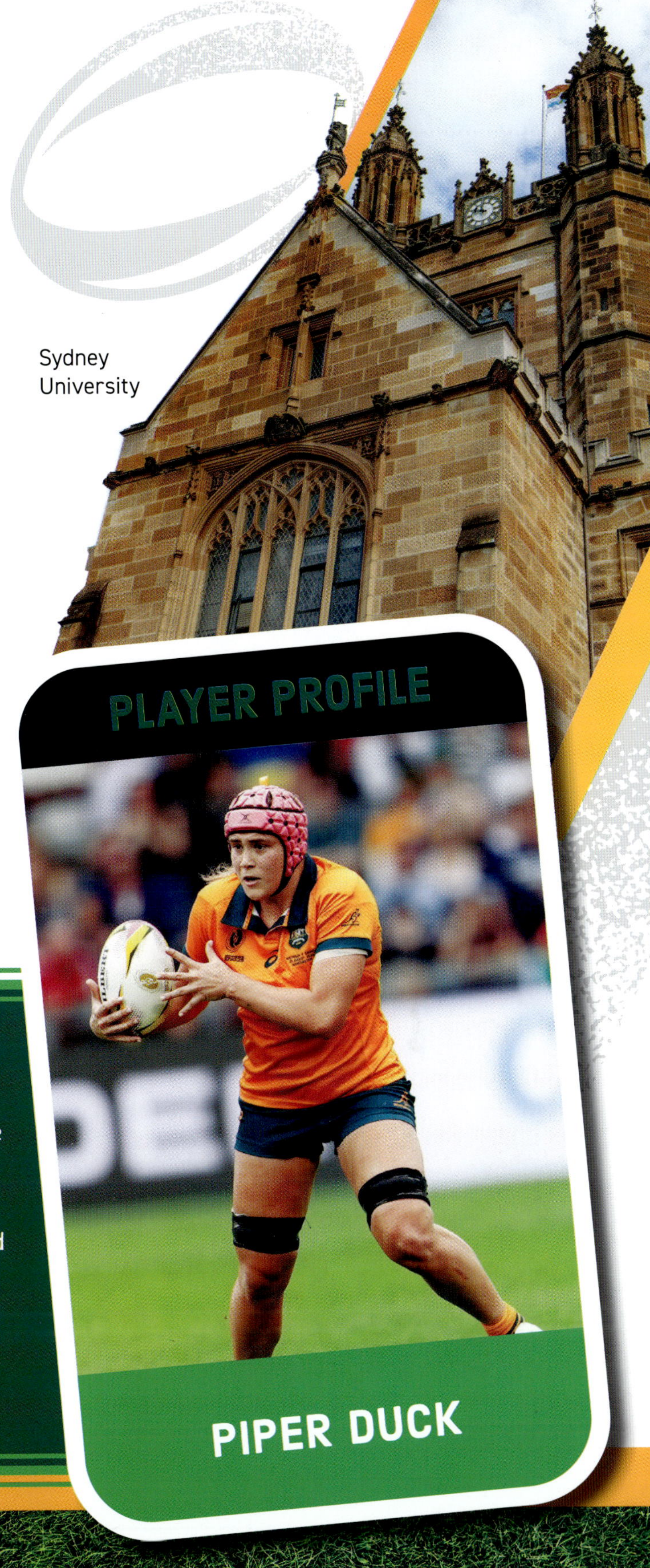

Sydney University

PLAYER PROFILE

Piper Duck is the youngest Waratahs captain for the Super Women's Competition. The 22-year-old captain has been committed to rugby from an early age, despite a limited access to pathways when she first started.

The Wagga-born back-rower progressed to School Girl 7s where she represented Barker College (2017) and played AON 7s for Sydney University, before attending her first 15s tournament with the Wallaroos A side in Fiji. While Duck represented Gordon at a junior level and Sydney University at a senior level, she has been committed to sky blue since 2020.

PIPER DUCK

INTERNATIONAL RECOGNITION

Australia Women's Rugby 15s & 7s players have become role models and ambassadors for the sport, inspiring a new generation of female athletes. Their achievements have encouraged young girls across Australia and the world to pursue rugby, contributing to the growth and diversification of the sport. The increased visibility of women's rugby has also led to greater media coverage and sponsorship opportunities, further elevating the game's profile.

The team's international recognition extends beyond their on-field accomplishments. They have been celebrated for their sportsmanship and commitment to fostering a positive and inclusive sporting culture. Their approach to the game emphasises respect, teamwork and resilience, values that resonate with audiences worldwide. The camaraderie and unity displayed by the teams have made them fan favourites, earning admiration from both rugby enthusiasts and casual spectators.

Teagan Levi is an emerging star of the 7s circuit after making her debut in Dubai, 2021.

The younger sister of Maddison Levi, the pair of sisters has fast become one of the best sibling partnerships in world sport. Like her sister, Teagan was a dancer before moving to touch football. Like her sister, she was drafted to the Gold Coast Suns in AFLW but instead opted to take up rugby.

Her inspiration growing up was teammate Charlotte Caslick, with Levi making her Olympic debut alongside Caslick and her sister Maddison at the Paris Games in 2024.

Teagan's journey into the world of rugby 7s is marked by a fierce determination and an unwavering commitment to her sport. From a young age, she was drawn to the physicality and teamwork inherent in rugby.

PLAYER PROFILE

TEAGAN LEVI

DOMESTIC COMPETITIONS

The women's rugby scene in Australia, particularly the rugby 15s and 7s, has been flourishing. Domestic competitions serve as the backbone of this burgeoning arena, providing a platform for athletes to improve their skills and showcase their talent.

Super Rugby Women's is a professional level competition organised by Rugby Australia. It is contested by four clubs from Australia and one club from Fiji, who play a single series of round-robin matches to determine the four participants of a single-elimination tournament.

Super Rugby Women's teams are: ACT Brumbies, Fijian Drua Women, NSW Waratahs Women, Queensland Reds Women, Western Force Women.

The rugby 7s format is known for its fast-paced and dynamic nature. It has its own set of domestic competitions that contribute to the development of the sport. The Aon University 7s Series is a standout competition, bringing together university teams from across Australia. The Aon Series has also been a stepping stone for many players who have gone on to represent Australia in international 7s tournaments.

NSW Waratahs playing against the Queensland Reds

SUPER RUGBY WOMEN'S COMPETITION

SEASON	CHAMPIONS	FINAL	RUNNERS-UP
2018	NSW Waratahs Women	16–13	Queensland Reds Women
2019	NSW Waratahs Women	8–5	Queensland Reds Women
2020	NSW Waratahs Women	– *	Queensland Reds Women
2021	NSW Waratahs Women	45–12	Queensland Reds Women
2022	Fijiana Drua Women	32–26	NSW Waratahs Women
2023	Fijiana Drua Women	38–30	Queensland Reds Women
2024	NSW Waratahs Women	50–14	Fijiana Drua Women
2025	NSW Waratahs Women	43–21	Queensland Reds Women

* The 2020 Women's Super Rugby season was cut short due to the Covid-19 lockdowns so there were no final scores. The NSW Waratahs were undefeated at the time and were crowned the champions.

FITNESS REGIMENS

The Australian Women's Rugby Sevens team is renowned for its rigorous fitness regimens, which are meticulously designed to enhance both individual and team performance on the field. The training programs are a blend of strength, speed, agility and endurance exercises, tailored to meet the high demands of rugby 7s. Each session is crafted with precision to ensure the athletes achieve peak physical condition, enabling them to maintain the intense pace required during matches.

Strength training forms a core component of the regimen, focusing on building muscle power and resilience. This involves a variety of exercises such as weightlifting, plyometrics and bodyweight workouts.

Tania Naden represents Australia at an international level, and plays for the Brumbies in the Super W competition. She stands out with her blistering pace and skill.

Tania first played rugby in 2017. She was asked by a friend to play for a local team in Canberra and was hooked from the first game.

She has been with the Brumbies since the inaugural Super W season in 2018, and made her first starting appearance in the second round of the 2022 season against the Melbourne Rebels.

In 2022, Tania played for the Australian Barbarians team against Japan, in the latter's Australian tour. She was named in the Wallaroos squad for the Rugby World Cup in New Zealand. She made her international debut against Wales at the World Cup and was selected again in the Wallaroos side for the 2023 Pacific Four Series, and the O'Reilly Cup. In 2024, Tania scored a hat-trick for the Brumbies against the Western Force in round five of the regular season.

COACHING TECHNIQUES

At the heart of effective coaching techniques lies an acute understanding of the players' individual strengths and weaknesses. Coaches meticulously analyse each athlete's performance, utilising video analysis and performance metrics to tailor training sessions that enhance skills and address areas needing improvement. This personalised approach ensures that each player is not only physically prepared but also mentally equipped to tackle the challenges posed by opponents.

Coaches employ various motivational techniques, from setting achievable goals to incorporating team-building activities that strengthen camaraderie. Understanding the unique motivations of each player, coaches craft individualised motivational strategies that inspire athletes to push their limits and strive for excellence.

PLAYER PROFILE

KAITLAN LEANEY

Kaitlan Leaney plays lock for Australia at an international level.

Leaney made her international debut for the Wallaroos against Fiji on 6 May 2022 at the Suncorp Stadium in Brisbane. She also played against Japan in a shocking 12–10 loss.

Leaney was named in Australia's squad for the 2022 Pacific Four Series in New Zealand. She was selected again in the Wallaroos squad for a two-test series against the Black Ferns at the Laurie O'Reilly Cup. She made the team again for the delayed 2022 Rugby World Cup in New Zealand.

In 2023, Leaney was selected in the Wallaroos side for the 2023 Pacific Four Series, and the O'Reilly Cup.

Isabella Nasser rapidly comes through the ranks in the Aussie 7s program after making her debut in Cape Town, 2022.

Nasser was inspired by the 2016 victory from the Women's team in Rio to go down the same path. She represented University of Queensland before moving to Sydney to enter the full-time program.

A mainstay since her debut, Nasser was impressive in her first Olympics campaign in Paris (2024), before she was awarded the captaincy ahead of the 2024-2025 season.

SKILL ENHANCEMENT

The foundation of skill enhancement lies in mastering the basics. For players, this begins with a focus on core skills such as passing, tackling and strategic kicking. These fundamental techniques are taught through rigorous practice sessions, where repetition and precision are key.

Beyond the basics, the development of advanced skills is essential for players aspiring to excel at the international level. This involves specialised training in areas such as spatial awareness, decision-making and the ability to read the game. Players are encouraged to engage in situational drills that mimic real-game scenarios, fostering a deep understanding of how to respond effectively to various challenges on the field.

A crucial element of skill enhancement in Australian Women's Rugby Sevens is the integration of technology and data analytics. Video analysis plays a pivotal role, allowing players and coaches to review performances, identify areas for improvement and develop strategies for future matches. By dissecting footage of both their own games and those of their opponents, players gain valuable insights into tactics and techniques, enhancing their overall game intelligence.

The physical aspect of skill enhancement cannot be overlooked. Strength and conditioning programs are tailored to the unique demands of rugby 7s, focusing on building endurance, speed and agility.

Siokapesi Palu competed for Australia at the 2021 Rugby World Cup in the Wallaroos in 2022. Palu was named in the Australian national team for a two-test series against the Black Ferns for the O'Reilly Cup. She was selected in the team for the delayed 2022 Rugby World Cup in New Zealand. She later featured in the Wallaroos WVX 2023 squad where she made the shift from the centres to the flanks.

PLAYER PROFILE

SIOKAPESI PALU

AUSTRALIAN TEAMS

2025 WOMEN'S RUGBY WORLD CUP 15s

Pool A	
England	 USA
 Australia	 Samoa

Pool B	
 Canada	 Scotland
 Wales	 Fiji

Pool C	
 Ireland	 New Zealand
 Spain	 Japan

Pool D	
 France	 Italy
 South Africa	 Brazil

2025 WALLAROOS SQUAD (15s)

Forwards: Katalina Amosa, Bree-Anna Browne, Annabelle Codey, Emily Chancellor, Piper Duck, Ashley Fernandez, Brianna Hoy, Asoiva Karpani, Lydia Kavoa, Kaitlan Leaney, Michaela Leonard, Ashley Marsters, Tania Naden, Bridie O'Gorman, Siokapesi Palu (captain), Faliki Pohiva, Adiana Talakai, Tabua Tuinakauvadra.

Backs: Lori Cramer, Waiaria Ellis, Georgina Friedrichs, Caitlyn Halse, Tia Hinds, Desiree Miller, Faitala Moleka, Manu'a Moleka, Layne Morgan, Trilleen Pomare, Cecilia Smith, Maya Stewart, Caitlin Urwin, Samantha Wood.

WOMEN'S 7s SQUAD 2025

Alysia Lefau-Fakaosilea, Bienne Terita, Bridget Clark, Charlotte Caslick, Demi Hayes, Faith Nathan, Heidi Dennis, Isabella Nasser, Kahli Henwood, Kaitlin Shave, Kiiahla Duff, Mackenzie Davis, Maddison Levi, Madison Ashby, Piper Simons, Ruby Nicholas, Sariah Paki, Sidney Taylor, Teagan Levi, Tia Hinds.

INTERNATIONAL MATCHES

The Australian Women's Rugby Sevens team has carved a formidable reputation on the international stage. From the outset, the Australian team has been a dominant force, consistently ranking among the top contenders in global tournaments. Their participation in the World Rugby Sevens Series has been particularly noteworthy. This annual series, comprising tournaments held across various countries, provides a platform for the team to demonstrate their prowess against the world's best. Each match in this series is a highly anticipated event, drawing fans and spectators eager to witness the thrilling display of athleticism and teamwork.

The Australian Women's team is renowned for their strategic depth and adaptability on the field.

The team's participation in the Olympics has been a highlight of their international journey. The inclusion of rugby 7s in the Olympic Games has elevated the sport's profile, providing an opportunity for the Australian team to showcase their talent on one of the world's biggest stages. Their gold medal victory at the 2016 Rio Olympics was an historic moment, solidifying their status as one of the premier teams in women's rugby 7s. International matches also serve as a platform for cultural exchange, with players interacting with teams from diverse backgrounds.

Team Australia preparing to play at the 2024 Paris Summer Olympics

Bienne Terita stands out in the world of Australian Women's Rugby Sevens not only for her athletic prowess, but also for her strategic mind. She is a dual threat, which makes her a formidable opponent.

Her eyes are sharp and calculating, always anticipating the next move. Her ability to read the game and adapt on the fly is a skill that sets her apart, a skill that has been nurtured through years of dedication and an unyielding passion for the sport. The impact of Bienne Terita on Australian Women's Rugby Sevens extends beyond her individual contributions. She embodies a spirit that inspires countless young athletes across the nation, particularly young women who see a reflection of their own potential in her.

PLAYER PROFILE

BIENNE TERITA

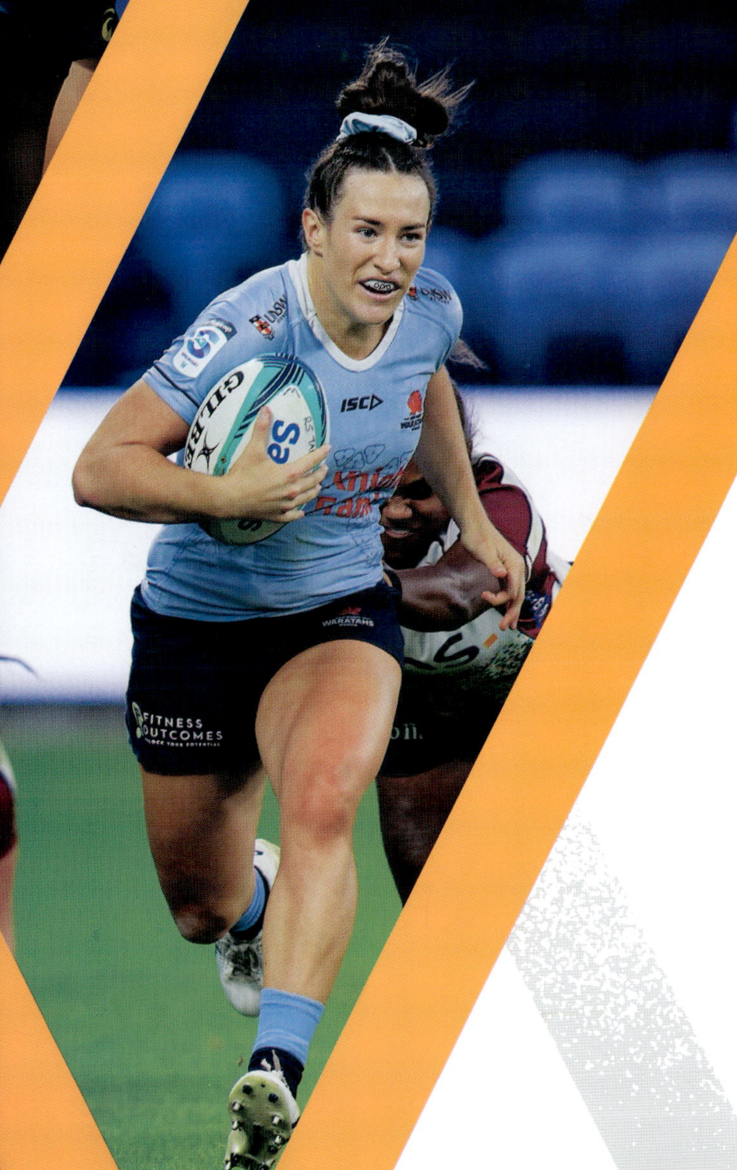

PHYSICAL BENEFITS

Rugby is a full-body workout that significantly boosts muscular strength and endurance. The sport involves tackling, scrummaging and mauling, which require immense physical strength and power. Regular training and matches help develop core strength, as well as upper and lower body muscles.

Flexibility and agility are other crucial physical benefits gained from playing rugby. The game demands quick directional changes, sudden accelerations and deft footwork, which enhance players' flexibility and agility. These attributes are vital for injury prevention and contribute to a player's ability to perform complex movements with ease. Enhanced flexibility also aids in maintaining a full range of motion in the joints, reducing the likelihood of strains and sprains.

Georgina Friedrichs is an Australian rugby 7s and union player. She has represented Australia in 7s and 15s internationally and competed at the 2021 Rugby World Cup in New Zealand. She also plays for the NSW Waratahs in the Super W competition.

Friedrichs made her debut for the Australian 7s team at the 2016 Canada Sevens in Langford.

In 2019, she switched to 15s and made her debut for Queensland Women against the Brumbies in the Super W season.

Friedrichs made her international test debut for the Australian 15s team on 6 May 2022 against Fiji. She was named in Australia's squad for the 2022 Pacific Four Series in New Zealand. She was also called up to the Wallaroos squad for a two-test series against the Black Ferns at the Laurie O'Reilly Cup.

In 2023, Georgina was named as the Wallaroos Player of the Year for 2022. She was selected in the Wallaroos side for the 2023 Pacific Four Series, and the O'Reilly Cup. She scored a try against the USA and featured in her side's loss to Canada.

MATCH DAY

The day of the game starts with light jogging before the team is taken through a matchday program by the fitness staff. The program is designed to 'rev' the players, without straining them. Our top players are now ready to take the field and put in 100% effort.

YOU ARE WHAT YOU EAT

All sports people pay special attention to their diet. A top player requires a diet that builds stamina and dietitians will work out a menu for each player. All the major food groups are represented in the diet program, with a variation towards match day when carbohydrates are increased to provide the extra energy required.

ICONS

The Australian Women's Rugby Sevens team, affectionately known as the "Aussie 7s," has become synonymous with success and innovation.

Key figures within the team have emerged as icons, inspiring young girls across the nation to pick up a rugby ball and dream big. Among them, players like Charlotte Caslick have become household names, celebrated for their electrifying runs and tactical brilliance. Their efforts have not only elevated the profile of women's rugby, but have also contributed to broader societal change.

Tui Ormsby is a former Australian rugby union player who made her international debut in 1997 against the United States. Ormsby competed in the 1998, 2002 and the 2010 Women's Rugby World Cups. She became the first Australian player to compete in four Rugby World Cups when she was named in the Wallaroos squad for the 2014 World Cup in France.

The success of the Australian Women's Rugby Sevens team is a story of teamwork and camaraderie. The bond shared by these athletes is evident in their seamless coordination during matches and their mutual support off the field.

Charlotte Caslick

Cheryl McAfee

TRAILBLAZER

Cheryl McAfee was the first captain of both the 7s and 15s World Cups for Australia. Under her leadership, her teams won the inaugural 7s in Dubai in 2008 plus third in the 15s World Cups in Surrey, England in 2010. Cheryl has also been included in the world rugby hall of fame, the first for an Australian female player.

RUGBY 7s RULES

Each team consists of seven players, as opposed to the traditional fifteen, and the matches are played over two halves of seven minutes each, with a brief halftime interval. The scoring system mirrors that of rugby union, with tries, conversions and penalty goals contributing to the team's total score. A try, worth five points, is scored when a player successfully grounds the ball in the opponent's in-goal area. Conversions, which follow a try, offer the opportunity to add two additional points. Conversions in rugby 7s must be taken as drop-kicks, adding an element of skill and precision under time pressure. Penalties and drop goals, each worth three points, provide further scoring opportunities.

Set pieces, such as scrums and lineouts, are simplified in 7s. Scrums involve three players from each team and are used to restart play after minor infringements. Lineouts occur when the ball goes out of play, with teams competing to regain possession through a throw-in.

Drop-kick conversion

RUGBY 15s RULES

The field dimensions for women's rugby are the same as men's rugby. Both versions of the game are played on a rectangular field that measures 100 metres in length and 70 metres in width. The goalposts are identical in both men's and women's rugby, consisting of two H-shaped posts.

Women's rugby uses the same standard rugby ball, which is oval.

Goalpost

Rugby ball

SCORING AND BASIC RULES

A try, which is worth five points, is awarded when a player successfully grounds the ball in the opponent's in-goal area. A conversion kick following a try is worth two points, while a penalty kick and a drop goal are each worth three points.

Scrums and lineouts are essential aspects of rugby. In women's rugby, scrums are often less forceful, with an emphasis on safety and technique.

In lineouts, which occur when the ball goes out of bounds, lifters are not allowed to lift their teammates above horizontal, ensuring safety during lineouts.

Women's rugby can be just as physical and intense as men's rugby.

Scoring a try

Conversion kick

Lineout

Scrum

RED AND YELLOW CARDS

In rugby 7s, any player who commits an offence – foul play – may be shown a yellow card and suspended from the game for two minutes without replacement. Offences include obstruction, unfair play, repeated infringements, dangerous play and misconduct which is prejudicial to the game. Receiving a yellow card is known colloquially as being sent to the "sin bin". If that player later commits another yellow-card offence, the player will be shown a red card and be sent-off.

Pulling or grabbing a player by their hair is regarded as foul play.

Referee showing a yellow card

FOUL PLAY

A player who commits foul play must either be cautioned, suspended or sent off.

OBSTRUCTION

When a player and an opponent are running for the ball, neither player may charge or push the other except shoulder-to-shoulder.

A player must not intentionally prevent an opponent from tackling or attempting to tackle the ball-carrier.

A ball-carrier must not intentionally run into an off-side team-mate to obstruct the opposition.

PENALTY

Unfair play

A player must not intentionally infringe any law of the game. The sanction for unfair play is a free kick for the opposing side.

Dangerous play

Players must not do anything that is reckless or dangerous to others including leading with the elbow or forearm, or jumping into, or over, a tackler.

Dangerous play in a scrum

A front-row player must not intentionally lift an opponent off their feet or force the opponent upwards out of the scrum.

A front-row player must not intentionally collapse a scrum.

Dangerous play in a ruck or maul

A player must not intentionally collapse a ruck or a maul.

DIAGRAM OF THE PLAYING FIELD

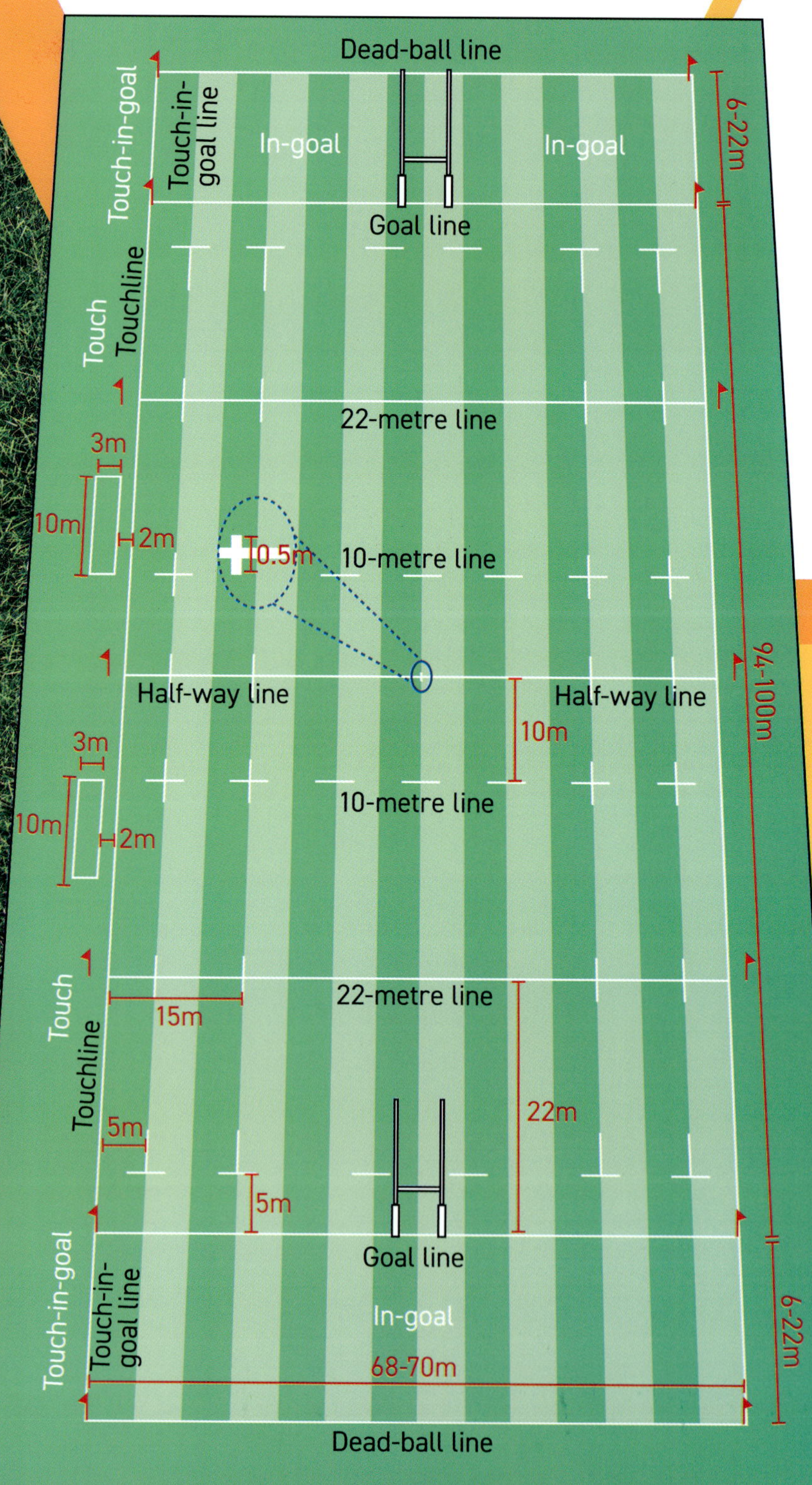

PLAYER POSITIONS 7s

Seven players from each team take their positions, each with roles as distinct as they are vital. Three forwards, and behind them, four backs, who are the architects of movement. The scrum-half acts as the pivotal link between the forwards and the backs. The fly-half, another key figure, is the playmaker, responsible for directing the attack. The centres, usually two, are versatile athletes who balance the dual responsibilities of defence and attack. Finally, the fullback stands as the last line of defence. This position demands exceptional field vision and the ability to make decisive runs, often turning defence into attack with a single, swift movement.

PLAYER POSITIONS 15s

Forwards

1 Loosehead Prop
2 Hooker
3 Tighthead Prop
4 & 5 Second Row Lock Forwards
6 Blindside-Flanker
7 Openside Flanker
8 Back Row Forward

Backs

9 Scrum-Half
10 Fly-Half
11 Left Wing
12 Inside Centre
13 Outside Centre
14 Right Wing
15 Fullback

KEY POINTS

Australian women's rugby, both the 15s and 7s formats, stand as pillars of athletic prowess and cultural significance. The distinction between these two forms of rugby is not just in the number of players or the duration of the game, but also in the style of play, tactical approaches and the spirit they encapsulate. Australian women's rugby has carved out a unique niche in the global sports arena, with its teams recognised for their skill, determination and strategic brilliance.

The 15s, or the traditional format, demands a high level of endurance and strategic planning, with each player performing specific roles that contribute to the team's overall performance. The Wallaroos have shown remarkable growth and development over the years, with their matches often exemplifying a perfect blend of strength, agility and tactical acumen.

In contrast, the 7s format is a fast-paced, high-energy spectacle that demands quick thinking and rapid execution. The 7s game is often seen as a test of individual brilliance as much as team cohesion, with players needing to adapt swiftly to the fast-changing dynamics on the field.

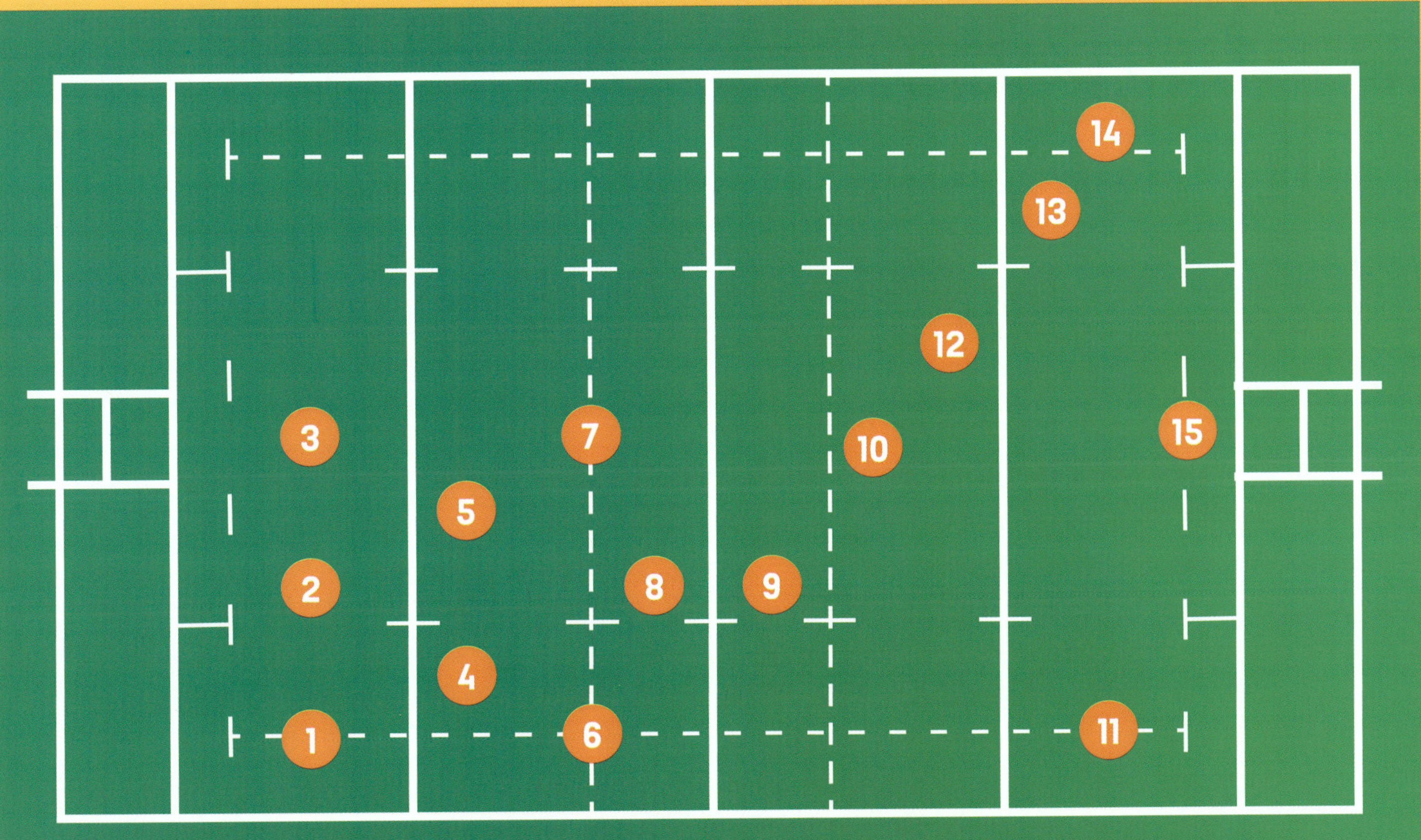

Maya Stewart plays for the Wallaroos internationally and for the NSW Waratahs in the Super W competition. She represented Australia at the delayed 2021 Rugby World Cup in New Zealand.

Stewart began her rugby career with the Nelson Bay Gropers, before moving to the Hunter Wildfires and then eventually making her way to the Waratahs in the Super W competition.

In 2021, Stewart scored four tries against the Queensland Reds in the opening game of the Super W season and made the squad for the Rugby World Cup in New Zealand.

She started 2023 with a brace of tries, and she helped her side win against Fiji.

In 2024, she scored in her sixth straight Test, and broke Tricia Brown's all-time record of 13 career tries.

She was crowned Wallaroos Player of the Year at the Rugby Australia Awards in October 2024.

ELITE TRAINING PROGRAMS

In women's rugby, the path to excellence is paved with rigorous and specialised training programs that cater to both the 15s and 7s formats. These elite training programs are meticulously designed to produce the skills, agility and strategic understanding necessary for athletes to excel on the international stage. At the core of these training programs is the aim of developing players who are not just physically fit but also mentally resilient, and capable of making split-second decisions in high-pressure situations.

Skill development is another cornerstone of these elite programs. Players engage in drills that refine their passing, tackling and ball-handling abilities. Coaches emphasise the importance of precision and accuracy.

In addition to the physical and tactical aspects, these programs place a strong emphasis on mental conditioning. Players are equipped with techniques to enhance focus, resilience and confidence. Mental toughness training helps athletes manage stress and maintain composure, particularly during critical moments in a match.

Moreover, nutrition and recovery are integral components of the training regimen. Athletes receive guidance on maintaining a balanced diet that supports their physical demands and promotes optimal performance. Recovery protocols, including physiotherapy and rest periods, are carefully managed to ensure players remain in peak condition and minimise the risk of injury.

HEAD WORK

It is just as important to have a sound mental program as it is to have a program for the body. Players can develop doubts and anxieties about their performance that can spoil their game. Rugby players listen to motivational speakers who can psych them up for a big match. They attend clinics that teach relaxation, and they learn to think in a positive way about their skills. Some players practise actualisation, which involves thinking about performing well in the hope that it will translate to improved natural performance during the match.

INAUGURAL MAJOR SPONSORS

Women's rugby is dependent on sponsors, who are needed for the tournament to flourish and expand. Some of the major sponsors for the 7s and 15s include Paper To Paper 2008-10 (7s and 15s) and Buildcorp 2016-present (15s).

GLOSSARY

conversion kick for goal following a try. A successful conversion awards you two points

evasion movement of the body designed to avoid a tackle

grassroots foundational or local level of a sport

kick-off start of play, when the ball is kicked forward from the centre

line-out after the ball goes out of bounds, players from both teams line up and the ball is thrown between them, creating a contest for possession

off-load when a player passes the ball to a teammate while being tackled

possession having control of the ball

ruck contest for possession of the ball in the phase of play. Players use their feet to move the ball or drive over it

scrum formation of players from each team to contest the ball after an infringement and after the ball leaves the field

tackle forcing a player in possession of the ball to the ground

try score achieved when the ball is legally carried over the goal line and touched on the ground

INDEX